" Yoga is as yoga does.
There's no in between.
You're either with it all the way,
or you blow the scene. "

- Elvis, *Easy Come, Easy Go*

Musings

01 Space
02 Wisdom of the body
03 Asana's journey
04 Elementals
05 The twist
06 Who are you?
07 The necklace
08 Today I am a student
09 Drishti
10 Yoga nidra savasana

Morsels

11 Take your time
12 Who knows?
13 Nothing
14 Every
15 Your practice
16 I can't breathe
17 My guru
18 Like life
19 The edge
20 Stay
21 Where is the fear?
22 Kat's koan

Mirth

23 Seeker's lament
24 On the mat
25 Practice, practice, practice
26 More and less
27 Swami rap
28 The meditation blues
29 Exquisite exhale

Meanderings

30 Human doing
31 The rush
32 Who
33 My heart is the moon
34 Pilgrim
35 A big silence
36 The potter
37 I am a corpse
38 Sweet loneliness
39 The thread
40 Heart of the lotus

Yoga has practiced me for forty years.

My students have taught me for twenty. In celebration of this magnificent journey, I offer these forty poetic observations - some playful, some, profound - all springing from the "heart of the lotus".

I have separated my work into four sections:

Musings explores the process.
Morsels provides juicy little bites that I share with my students.
Mirth reminds us not to take any of this or ourselves too seriously.
Meanderings invites a deeper, more mystical inquiry.

Any seeker can enjoy the gifts of Voices from the Mat. These verses could be shared by an instructor as an opening meditation or as a lovely close to final relaxation. Reading them alone, a student may find they encourage clarity and inspiration. Even someone who's never been "on the mat" will find this collection thought-provoking and entertaining.

I've observed the world through the soft yet focused eyes of yoga for four glorious decades and been both enriched and humbled by what I've experienced. With pleasure and joy, I share my vision with you.

Namaste,

Kat.

MUSINGS

Space

Though seemingly of earth,
we're mostly space.
Like wind through leaves
or the vibration place
of particles so small,
they are but a concept
in a realm of possibility.

A splatter of stars spasm
in a velvet void.
Whole universes, merely motes
in an expanse of the abyss.
Of this non-stuff, we rise.

So, inhale into Infinity
and breathe out - out -
Further out.
Find space between your hipbones
and your lowest ribs.
Between your ribs, breathe room.
Probe undiscovered emptiness
twixt shoulders and your ears,
your brows,
These new frontiers.
Untangle all the places that are caught.
Can you find space

Between

Your

Thoughts?

Wisdom of the body

There is a wisdom in the bones.
The body knows
and chooses Life.
Why don't we listen?
Intuition
of the gut,
A thousand answers in the lungs.
If we could hear
the sage advice of flesh and blood.
The body's way is clean and clear.

Why is it, then, that
we choose fear?

Asana's journey

Cautiously, I seek the boundary of my ease,
breath by breath by shallow breath.
The forest edge invites me in.
I let my exhale deepen
in surrender to that steady guide.

There, through the trees, I see a light,
and past the light,
a woods.
The light is soft.
The forest, deep and warm.

Beyond that light,
another wood.
Another light beyond.

I am the light,
the moody woods,
the boundary
and the way.

I am asana's journey.

Standing Poses teach me patience.
Forward Bends, humility.
The Twist appreciates how far I've come.
Inversions welcome other ways to see.

Salutations let me glide.
A Side Bend helps me find my breath.
In Child's Pose, I feel tender.
Back Bends urge me, "Trust the ride."
Savasana, surrender.

A Downward Dog inspires length.
Without focus, I could never hold a Tree.
Chaturanga knows my weakness
and my strength.
In Meditation, I learn me.

The twist

The swami in the twist
reminds me that I rise up from my roots.

Find guidance in my gut.

Face forward.

Gaze back.

The swami in the twist
reminds me to be where I am,
but honor where I was,

And forgive it.

Who are you?

Who are you?
Have we met?
You with the root-bound belly
Strangled calves
Petrified knees.

It's a pity -
So much unexplored space.

Let me take you by the breath
and lead you into Non-Judgment.

Or perhaps, a little further,
into Love.

The necklace

A perfect strand of asanas
strung on a golden thread of breath.
No clasp.
No knot.
A necklace of great salutation
welcoming you to yourself.

But, could you wear it?
Would you dare?
Do you have the patience?

It doesn't match your ego suit.
It wouldn't go with haste.
It clashes terribly with judgment and with pride.

But, perhaps in some forgotten drawer,
you find a small Desire.
Curiosity will do.
Try on the necklace now.

Oh my,
You look Divine.

Today I am a student.
This emptiness surprises me
with wonderment and joy.
My years of "practice" fall away.
Today I am a student.

The jaded eye blinks firmly shut.
The Inner Eye awakens -
Beholding like a wriggling babe
delighted in discovering her own two feet.
Today I am a student.

Each breath that never was before
releases me from judgment, habit and result
that may be hiding there between my blades,
my stoic jaw, my furrowed brow.
Today I am a student.

And today

And today

And today

I am a student.

Drishti

Let your eyes go soft.
Take in what's around you.
Take out what's inside.

The gaze is on the breath.
Not tight and sharp
like the eagle on her prey,

Not quick and fearful like the hare.

But light and steady and serene.

There may be wetness on the brow
or fire in the limbs,
but all will accomplish itself
breath by breath

As soft eyes see the way.

I bless my feet that have taken me so far.
And I let them go.
I bless my knees, for they have taught me humility.
And I let them go.
I bless my legs that have encouraged me to take a stand.
And I let them go.
I bless my hips for opening a world of sensuality and play.
And I let them go.
I bless my belly for its guidance.
And I let it go.
I bless my lungs for their breath and my ribs for they hold my
heart.
And I let them go.
I bless my spine for its support.
And I let it go.
I bless my shoulders, which have born so much and complained so
little.
And I let them go.
I bless my arms that have embraced and comforted.
And I let them go.
I bless my hands for their creativity and compassion.
And I let them go.
I bless my neck that has held my head high.
And I let it go.
I bless my lips for their teaching words and kind intentions.
And I let them go.
I bless my eyes that have seen so much and connected so deeply.
And I let them go.
I bless my mind that has shown me the way.
And I let it go.

And I let letting go, go.

MORSELS

Take your time

Take your time.

If you don't, somebody else will.

Who knows?

Change is slow.

While you're waiting,

why not like what you've got?

Who knows?

You might like it so much,

you won't want to change it.

Nothing

What is breath?

Breath is air.

Air is nothing.

Fill the empty space inside with

Nothing.

Every

Every pose is Mountain Pose.

Every breath reveals your truth.

Every hamstring stretch is an opening

for self-forgiveness.

Your practice

Let your practice be an intention,

not a demand.

I can't breathe

I can't breathe.

My chest is held captive by my heart.

My guru

My guru this.

My guru that.

My guru speaks in the space

between the breaths,

the distance between the bones,

and the silence between the thoughts.

Like life

Asana practice is like life.

You don't want to get to the end too fast.

The edge

Where is your edge?

Let the exhale tell you -

not the ego.

Stay

Stay inside your breath.

Where is the fear?

Where is the fear?

There –

Hiding between your shoulder blades.

There -

Where your wings used to be.

Kat's koan

Be more interested in what you are doing now,

than what you are not doing now.

Holistically speaking, you feel like Swiss cheese.
You've been Rolfed 'til your psyche is weak in the knees.

You've been hypnotized, ionized, and biofed, and Kava
does nothing but go to your head.

You've found It with EST, and you've lost it with T.M.
You chant with your mala beads a.m. and p.m.

Your beard's at your navel. Your Pranas are faded.
Your armpit hair's grown so at last you can braid it.

Your Tarot's been read and your aura's been measured.
Your feet have been punctured; your back, acupressured.

Your flip-flops are vegan, your mouth, gluten-free. You're Vatta,
you're Pitta – heck, maybe all three!

You've learned to say "quinoa", "acai", and "bulgur".
You cleanse with your neti pot (not to sound vulgar).

Your hot tub is solar. You read Kubler-Ross, and after
Tofurkey, you use dental floss.

Your clothes are recycled, not Bonwit or Saks. You eat senna
and psillium, never ExLax. You've worn through your Toe Shoes
and seven backpacks,

But, Depak forgive you, you just can't relax!

Stay on the mat.
It's tempting, though,
to fly away -
Perhaps to weigh
the words you said to So-and-So
or wonder what's for lunch today.
But stay
on
the
mat.
Find wonderment between your toes.
Who knows?
You may enjoy a trip
inside your hip.
Listen.
There's a whisper in your bones.
"Come home."
"Come play."
Stay
on the mat.

Just that.

I hate you.
Hamstrings like piano wires.
Buttocks locked like precious treasure.
Backbone bound by too many years,
Fears.
I hate you.
I don't want to slow down.
I don't want to "let go".
I don't want to breathe.
I can't.
I won't.
I should.
I
Surrender.
Okay. There.
But just this once.
I already paid my fourteen bucks.
But then, I'm outta here.
Here?
Where's here?
Here is now.
That's where I am.
I am.
I Am.

More and less

Less talk,
More breath.

Less breath,
More silence.

Less silence,
More thought.

Less thought,
More being.

Less being,
More nothing.

Now you have something to say.

Swami rap

Nadi
Nauli
Pranayama
Mukti
Yogi
Om
Samsara

Karma
Dharma
Maya
Mudra
Yoni
Shakti
Kama Sutra

Guru
Chela
Satya
Cit

Hatha Yoga

Yeah, that's it.

I can't meditate.
I know I can't. I've tried it.
It's tougher than my income tax.
It's harder than a diet.

I sit up straight. My eyes are crossed.
I pray that no one sees me.
My anal mouth is grinning.
Where the heck's my Kundalini?

I'll meditate by lying down.
I'm trying to unwind,
but what I'd really like to do
is shoot my monkey mind.

Okay, I'm on my zafu now.
I've got the candle lit.
My crystal's hanging round my neck.
I'm all prepared to sit.

Ganesh is on the alter,
and the Yanni's playing soft.
I take a mighty cleansing breath.
The incense makes me cough.

I try it now with open eyes.
I'm staring at my yantra.
It's gotta be more fun than this.
Oh, heck, I'm trying Tantra.

Exquisite exhale

29

We're People of the Inhale
Bored.
Hoarding.
Taking in without a question
More
Technology,
The latest trends,
The Pokes, the Tweets,
The Facebook Friends.

Obesity of obsolescence.
Blog bloat.
Intergestion.
Eyeballs spinning,
Faces pale.
Thumbs arthritic.
Now,
Exhale.

"What's the purpose?" you might
ask.
Where are you going?
Why are you leaving?
Try this as a multi-task —
Can you breathe
and know you're breathing?
Gasp.

That's it.
Now let it go.
Don't pant.
Make space in your
unconsciousness.
Exhale until you can't
exhale
any
more.

Then wait.
The Inhale knows its way.
Bask in the luxury of doing
Nothing
Letting out.
A fine staycation.
Receive the gift of
E
  x
   h
    a
     l
      a
       t
        i
         o
          n.

MEANDERINGS

Human doing

30

If you're a doer,
do without.
Be brave.
Be bored.
Plunge into that excruciating void of idleness.
Muck around in a bit of death.
Let it bind you for awhile -
drag on your limbs and brain like a sleepwalker.
Be the victim of your self-imposed inertia.
Don't fight back.
Don't make excuses.
Don't DO anything.
Sit.
In time, you will be baptized by your own tears —
Rinsed in emptiness.
Exhausted fully.
Now,
There,
Inside.
Can you feel it?
The heartbeat of God.

The rush

31

What's the rush?
Why so fast?
Another January, June, July.

Everywhere I run, I slam into a brick me.

So, I breathe – reluctantly.

I slow down.
I slow down.

I

slow

down.

The brick softens.
The grout melts.
I flow like a warm red river
that gently rocks me downstream.
So slowly that I can see grasses
dancing on the far shore.
Feel the dragonfly's heartbeat
Hear the sigh of the snail.

This is the rush.

Who

32

Yoke the oxen.
Harness the mind.
Who reins behind?
Who drives the beasts?

The blade
plows deep the sorry clay,
callous from fear,
yet fertile still
and thirsting for
the drench of Love.
Who is the Tiller?

The field lies bare.
The seeds await the Planter's hand.
The seeds of what?
Of peace? Of greed?
Serenity? Need?
Who is the Planter?

Who drives the oxen?
Tills the field?
Who plants the seed anew?
Who tends the land?
And who, the yield?

Who is this?

It is you.

My heart is the moon

My heart is the moon,

So fat and full.
Encircling my soul.

I offer half-light
Cool
Remote
Enough that you may find your way.

And as the moon reflects the sun,
so my heart mirrors you,
my Love,
The Infinite Divine.

Pilgrim

Go to India?
Why?
I come with myself wherever I go.
Is my baggage any lighter in Jaipur?
I fly on the wings of fear right here at home.
What is in India
that I don't visit every morning in my glass?
My pilgrimage is here.
Inside.
Every day with every thought.
My guru is the breath.
The asana.
The practice that slows me down enough
to know who I am,
and who I think I am.
I am the lesson and the blessing.
Awakened and still dreaming.
I am the poor and hungry.
I am the swami and the student.

I am India.

A big silence

Cultivate a big Silence.
Sow it in your spine.
Feed it with the breath.
Water with compassion.
Let it grow so big
and loud,
that you can no longer
hear yourself think.

What a harvest that will be.

The potter

The potter lifts his lump of clay
and slaps it on the spinning wheel,
As I sit musing on my mat, a dervish of ideas
Ideas
Ideas
Ideas.

The potter's strong and skillful palms
now center the slick loam,
As does the breath control my slippery mind
My mind
My mind.

The potter plunges to the core
and stretches thin the sides.
As does my flesh expand in asana divine
Divine.

The potter's work, fixed to the earth,
stays open at the top.
As, mindfully, do I.

The potter's vase, or jug, or bowl
may serve a useful purpose.
As,
Consciously,
May
I.

I am a corpse

37

I am a corpse that walks -
Extinguished.
Exhausted.
Dead to my body.
My mind, a thousand silver butterflies.

I warily inflate the grey balloon,
and then I let it go.

Again.

And then again.

The pink returns.

My spine unfurls.

The Monarchs settle on a branch of breath.

Their luster glistens in my eyes.

Sweet loneliness

Be still.

Wrap yourself in your sweet loneliness.

Let it be a comfort not a bane.

Companions come.

Companions go.

There is no one more True than this friend,

Your sweet Loneliness.

Don't be afraid of nothing

Don't be afraid of Nothing
when you see it grinning up at you
from deep inside an empty bowl
or lurking on a wall devoid of art.

Don't be afraid of Nothing
when you're confronted with
a day of simple wandering –
of lapping up bright sunbeams
or of listening to crocus growing
and the clickering of crow.

When your sentences are stale air
And your silences profound.

Don't be
afraid
of

Heart of the lotus

40

I am born of mud and dung,
Of murk and mire deep.
Thick, primordial, suckling blind
from the soft, dark underbreast of Sleep.

Through twilight tides,
I sway and weave in eddies of emotion.
I blithely heed the liquid pull of my own mind
while innocently unaware of Lethe's sly devotion.

But quietly, and far below,
An urge. A tender bud begins to grow.
An ever-drawing-upward thrusting
out of the Shadow surge into the Light.
I fight to bathe in Heaven's gaze.

Elusive longings now insist, and I persist
until I pierce the surface of my past.

This world of water slips away,
and I emerge at last – a creature of the sky.

Pale arms embrace the ardent sun.
My fingertips blush pink
as I unveil what has been shy -
that golden center of my soul.

Now surely-rooted in the Earth,
my Spirit plays in Light,
I am my Chosen One –
The Jewel.

Om mani padme hum.

ABOUT THE AUTHOR

Kat Sawyer has been a student, practitioner and teacher of yoga for over four decades in both her native California and now in New Mexico.

She credits Ganga White, founder of vinyasa flow, as a mentor and inspiration.

Her clients range from celebrities to corporations such as The Golden Door, Sebastian International, and The Four Seasons Resorts.

She describes her yogic way as guiding students gently and playfully into a Life After Breath.

A longtime stage and film actress, Sawyer has also proved conversant with the pen, having published articles in *Ms. Fitness*, *The Artists Magazine*, and *Cosmopolitan*, among others.

Most recently, she has built a reputation as a coveted and award-winning landscape painter. Known for her play of light and shadow, her work can be seen in galleries in Santa Fe and throughout California.

Dear Reader,

If you enjoyed this work, please consider sharing a review on Amazon. com

Namaste,

Kat.

Made in the USA
San Bernardino, CA
16 October 2015